Fritz

The Adventures Begin

Rose Tooley Gamblin

MRG Publishing

A Division of MRG Media Inc

Since 2012

This book was
Edited by Vaughn Jennings
Designed by Rose Gamblin
Illustrated by Rose Gamblin
Cover by Michael Gamblin
Typeset: Times Roman 16/24

PRINTED IN U.S.A.

Gamblin, Rose Tooley, 1956 -

Summary: The kids want a dog, and after some interesting circumstances, they get a misshapen dachshund that the pet shop rejected. One adventure after another happens to the Dory family, with Fritz in the middle of them all.

ISBN 979-8-9991719-0-0

Other Books by Rose Tooley Gamblin

Like a Little Child   Safe Kids
Bill's Lunch   Fritz Finds a Way
The Birthday Party
Baby Moses
Esther the Brave Queen
Joash the Boy King

Dedication

Dedicated to, first my children, who each evening begged for one more story (dory), hence the last name 'Dory'. Then my grandchildren grew up hearing these stories, and now they can share them with their children. Next, all the schools and churches that have listened to these stories have encouraged me to write them down. Last, I'd like to mention the school-age children of Mt. Nebo United Methodist Christian Learning Center. They have been the final inspiration to share these stories with children everywhere so that they, too, can enjoy Fritz, the true adventures of a wonder dog.

Contents

1 FANGS 1

2 Hoped-For Dog.................................15

3 WHAT'S THAT?..............................28

4 Zzzzzzzzip 38

5 The Pit...51

6 The Spark...62

7 The Peanut.......................................72

8 The Man..86

9 The Field Trip................................102

10 The Hood 116

11 The Big Stink 128

12 The Creek....................................138

13 Stuck 149

Epilogue..162

Analogous Learning........................163

ACKNOWLEDGMENTS

I would like to acknowledge my husband, Michael Gamblin, who worked tirelessly on both the book cover and the formatting of the manuscript.

1 FANGS

The creature sprawled out across the warm granite boulder. The sun felt good after the winter's sleep. Then he sensed the vibrations. He flicked his forked tongue, tasting the sound. It grew louder and louder and stopped not far from him. For a moment, his yellow, silted eyes glinted in the sun, and then he slithered off the boulder and disappeared among the rust-colored pine needles that carpeted the forest floor.

The Dorys were on their first-ever camping trip on a late Friday afternoon. Jenny was the oldest, followed by Johnny, James, and Fritz, the puppy.

"It's perfect." Mom breathlessly took in the pastoral scene with its babbling brook, tall pines, and needle-carpeted floor.

"Let's play rock tag." Jenny dashed to a group of boulders. Soon, she and Johnny were jumping from one to the other while James cried,

"Up, up," and Fritz barked frantically.

Dad began setting up the pup tents, smiling as he remembered his wife's reaction to the thought of camping.

* * *

"Melba, we need to create some family memories by camping."

"Paul, bad idea, we don't have any camping equipment."

"Well, Melba, I know where I can get everything we need, cheap too."

Dad headed out to the VW van with a determined look. The van was white on top and red all around the sides, with a large, white VW in the front. The local churches had combined their resources so the Dorys would have dependable transportation and could use it as the school bus.

Dad opened the door, and all three children and Fritz jumped into the van. In just a few miles, the VW van pulled into Oroville and came to a stop in front of a dilapidated-looking brick building with a metal sign that read "*ARMY SURPLUS*."

The pungent odor of musty wool, mildewed canvas, and rusty metal greeted the group.

"How can I help you?" asked a skinny middle-aged man emerging from behind a red Formica-covered counter. Jenny and Johnny were mesmerized by the items in the glass case under the counter. There were shiny shells, guns, mess kits, and war medals neatly arranged on black velvet.

"I need some camping equipment," announced Dad.

"Well, you've come to the right place; here are the sleeping bags and some pup tents." The man motioned to some metal shelves that contained stacks of khaki green folded canvases with twine-looking bits and pieces of rope sticking here and there. Dad looked at the price tags. Selecting two pup tents, Dad put them under his arm and started going through the sleeping bags. He picked up three wool mummy bags (vintage from World War I) and two large canvas sleeping bags.

"The mummy bags will be for your kids. And these big ones will be for Mom and me,"

"We're getting some mommy bags."

"I wonder why they are called mommy bags."

"Do you think mommies slept in them during the war?"

"The word is 'mummy'," and they are called that because they have a head covering that makes you look like a mummy." Dad's explanation made perfect sense, except for one thing.

"What is a mummy?"

"It's a dead Pharaoh that has been mummified."

"What is a Pharaoh?"

"I'll tell you later." Dad guided the kids up to the counter and purchased two pup tents, two sleeping bags, three mummy bags, and a kerosene lamp.

"You all have a wonderful camping trip!" said the man as they left the store.

After a scenic uphill climb into the Wallowa Mountains, they discovered a beautiful campsite beside a little brook surrounded by tall lodgepole pine trees. Mom worked on getting a campfire going while Dad put up the tents. Each pup tent consisted of one rectangular piece of canvas, two poles, ropes, and stakes. Dad began by staking the canvas down to the ground. Slowly, he'd raise the tent by forcing the center poles up into the grommets as he moved back and forth between the front and the back, adjusting the poles and then the stakes. Perspiration beaded on his face. Once the tent was high enough, he crawled inside. The tent sagged in the middle, and he tried to remedy that by forcing the poles at each opposing opening with his body.

"Yay!" Jenny and Johnny yelled as the tent reached full height. But when Dad released the pressure, the whole tent sagged over him, creating a ghostly shape in the setting sun.

"Here, Paul, let me help you," Mom laughed. Moving the cast-iron skillet from the fire, she joined Dad. The children had often heard stories of how she'd

lived in a canvas tent during her young years. Together, they soon had both pup tents up and secured.

"OK, kids, it's time to collect some pine needles and fill the floor of your tent so you'll have a nice, soft bed." Jenny, Johnny, and James eagerly piled the needles into their tent and spread their mummy bags over them. Again, the serpent moved away from the needles, disturbed by their incessant talking. Soon it was time for supper and a bath. The mountain brook looked inviting.

"I'll beat you." Johnny began running toward the water, and Jenny raced after him. They both jumped in at the same time with a big splash, showering James, who started to cry.

"Hush," Mom scrubbed his little body. "Now dip down, and you'll be sparkling clean."

"Ill dddon't wwwant ttto bbbe bbbarkling clclclean!" James chattered. Mother plunged the little boy into the water, pulled him out, and wrapped him in a blanket. Jenny and Johnny were through with their icy bath and jumped out quickly into their cold pajamas.

"I'll beat you." Jenny ran to their tent and climbed into her mummy bag. Shivering and shaking, no one needed coaxing to get into bed. Mom crawled in behind them and prayed for each child. Then she left, giving them a stern command to go to sleep. Dad sat by the campfire, softly playing *Una Paloma Blanca* on his guitar. James brought Fritz closer and gently rubbed the little dog's ear; both fell quickly to sleep, but as Jenny lay and listened to the night sounds, her mind began to wander.

It began as a tingle but soon turned to

itchiness, then escalated to sheer torture as the needles reached through the wool and played *Pin-the-tail-on-the-donkey* on her skin.

"Jenny, are you awake?"

"Yes, this is very itchy."

"I know! Hey, Jenny, can you tell me a story?"

"Do you want to hear a story about where these mummy bags came from?" she asked.

"Not really," said Johnny, "I want a story about a horse."

"Too bad, I will tell you a story about my bag. It's that or nothing." With a sigh of resignation, Johnny cozied down into his bag. Any story would help take his mind off all this poking and itching.

* * *

"The soldiers had just landed on the

beach, and tomorrow would be the big day. They would storm the castle and release the American prisoners. A soldier named John had my mummy bag."

"Hey, that's my name. You can't use my name." Johnny whispered.

"OK, a soldier named Ray had my mummy bag, and a soldier named Mark had your mummy bag. They were best friends. The two soldiers were so exhausted that they welcomed the dry sand high on the seashore and settled into their mummy bags for some rest. Ray was just about asleep when Mark jabbed him.

'Hey, do you see that light from the castle?' Ray woke up with a start. From the top of the castle, a small light flickered so erratically that both soldiers almost ignored it; maybe it was just the reflection from the moon on a shiny rock. As they continued to watch the light, they began to see patterns: blink, blink, blink, dash, dash, dash, blink, blink, blink. Ray, who knew Morse Code, began translating for Mark. 'They say they're going to be executed in the morning.'

"We can't let that happen!" Exclaimed Mark. "We've come this far; we've gotten this close. What should we do?'"

* * *

Jenny paused in her storytelling. Dad had stopped playing his guitar, and she could hear him whispering to Mom. Johnny lay motionless in his mummy bag; deep sleep had won over the wool and needles. *I love camping,* Jenny thought as she drifted off.

"Time to wake up in the morning when the birds begin to sing." Mom sang from the campfire while stirring the eggs. *Wow, it was*

so hard to leave the cozy warmth of the tent.
Thought Jenny and then scurried with the
others out to a breakfast of scrambled eggs
and pancakes. They were rushing, so
anxious to get to the boulders.

"King of the mountain!" Johnny yelled
as he climbed the first one.

"King of this mountain!" Jenny yelled from
a higher boulder.

"Up, up!" cried James, his frustration
mounting as he tried and slipped at each
boulder. Fritz barked in excitement, following
the older children as they continued to jump
from boulder to boulder. Mom smiled; *yes,
Jenny would win for now, but someday, the
boys would be men, and they would win at
everything.*

It all happened so fast; he was tired of the stomping, the screaming, the barking; the children's voices drowned out his warning rattle. He struck and struck fast, aiming for the little human legs, but his fangs caught the face of the little dog instead and cut deep into the flesh. The forest hushed at the screams of Fritz's pain. He ran wildly around the boulders for a moment, all the time emitting a dog-awful cry. The children watched in terror as the large timber rattler slithered off into the dense needles and was gone.

2 Hoped-For Dog

Dad and Mom hurriedly packed up the campsite, and Jenny and John took down the tents. Fritz's cries lessened as he sank into unconsciousness. Tears streamed down James's face as he gently patted the dog. Even though Mom and Dad were so grateful that the little dog had taken the strike rather than their youngest child, they still felt sad for the children.

"We'll get down the mountain as fast as possible and get him to a vet," Dad assured them.

"It didn't even enter my mind that this kind of danger could be in such a lovely place." Mom's voice broke.

After throwing the last items in the back of the van, Dad turned and gently lifted the little dog into his arms.

"Jenny and Johnny, get in the middle seat. I will put Fritz across your lap so you can watch him." Dad laid the limp dog across their legs, and James crawled in the back and looked over the top of the seat. Jenny had Fritz's swelling head in her lap, and she gently stroked his ear. She could see the fang marks and the fresh blood that trickled down the dog's face.

"It's going to be OK," she whispered to Fritz. "We're going to get you to the doctor." There was no response from Fritz. His face was taking on a grotesque look as the swelling began to pull his skin away from his teeth.

"Is he still breathing?" Mom asked, turning around.

"I don't know. Nothing is moving." A warm

tear fell from Jenny's cheek and splashed on Fritz's shiny black coat.

"I'm sure the veterinarian will have some antivenom medication." Mom tried to sound optimistic. Jenny nodded, determined to stifle the sobs that threatened to choke off her breathing. Fritz was her special, hoped-for, begged-for, and prayed-for dog; her mind wandered to the events that led to Fritz becoming part of their family.

* * *

It was November 22, 1963, the last school day before the school's Thanksgiving Vacation. The teacher laid out a long piece of butcher paper and allowed the students to draw a mural. Jenny worked on developing a forest of pine trees; in her mind, they would become the most beautiful Christmas trees. Which reminded her, this year would be the best Christmas; she was praying for a puppy. Even though Dad and Mom gave several reasons they couldn't have a dog: too young, too large a responsibility, too expensive. But she had told Santa Claus and God, too. It was going to happen; she just knew it!

Ring, ring, ring. Jenny looked up from her tree painting. The two-room church school had a black phone that hung on the wall. The teacher, her mom, answered the phone and then started crying. John F. Kennedy, the president of the United States, had been assassinated. Some of the older girls cried, too. A somber group of students left for home and vacation that day. The next day, the Dorys loaded their Packard and went to Grandma and Grandpa's house in Portland, Oregon.

"We're going to have Thanksgiving dinner at Ray and Clarine's," Grandma announced as she welcomed each person. *Wow, that's going to be awesome, thought* Jenny. Her Uncle Ray and Aunt Clarine were considered the high-class members of the family. They and their two girls, Jan and Marilyn, owned their own home, had a nice car, and the girls had stylish clothes. Jan, the oldest, was just a few months older than Jenny.

"Now, remember your manners." Mom instructed the children as they jumped out of the van. Jenny remembered to take off her shoes as she entered the foyer.

"Do you want to see my room?" Jan asked. The two girls went to Jan's bedroom. Jenny had never seen anything so beautiful.

"You mean you don't share your room with Marilyn?" Jenny asked as she looked at the neat array of glass figurines. The single bed had a pink frilly bedspread with a matching canopy. It was hard to imagine having one's own room. She shared her room with both of her brothers. Jan went to a small dressing table and opened all the drawers so Jenny could see. The drawers were full of sparkling jewels and plastic cases of makeup.

"Wow, you wear make-up?" Jenny was amazed.

"No, it's just for play. Do you want some lipstick?" Jenny hesitated and then let Jan apply the bright red lipstick. It made her lips feel thick and sticky, and she blew some kisses into the air like she'd imagined the high-society ladies would do.

"Come and eat." The call from the dining room interrupted the girls' play. Everyone had a specific place to sit with real China, matching silverware, and name tags.

"Jenny, what's that on your lips?" Jenny paused in terror. She could tell by Dad's voice that she had done something wrong.

"Lipstick." She replied timidly.

"Go wash it off." Jenny obediently got down from the table and went to the bathroom. Her aunt Clarine hurried behind her with some paper towels.

"Don't feel bad." She assured Jenny. "You did nothing wrong. You are a beautiful girl with naturally beautiful red lips." The kind tone and soft touch of her aunt made her feel better. Someday, she'd have to find out what was so bad about lipstick. Jenny relaxed when the lunch conversation turned away from her and the evils of lipstick to the topic of the recent assassination.

Lunch was over, and Jenny hesitated to return to Jan's room; instead, she played with Aunt Clarine's dog, Pepsi. Pepsi was a purebred Dachshund and loved kids. Jenny imagined it would be the kind of dog she'd get someday.

"I was able to sell all of her puppies, well, almost all of her puppies, to the local pet store." Aunt Clarine said, "I think I will have her bred again." Uncle Ray rolled his eyes and then interjected.

"It's like this, the dog, the pet store rejected, has chewed the pool table and piano legs, pooped all over the floor, which reminds me, kids, would you like to go downstairs?" Jenny, Johnny, and James followed their uncle to the basement. As their eyes got accustomed to the darkness, they were surprised to see upholstery yarn strung out from the pool table legs around the piano pedals and across the room; they were even more surprised when their Uncle Ray began yelling.

"You stupid, no-good-for-nothing dog!" He grabbed a broom and started after the little black puppy, who dashed, hiding behind the couch. Jenny could see big holes in the sofa, and a bit of fabric was still held tightly in the little dog's mouth as he peeked and shuddered from his hiding place. Pausing momentarily in his rage, Uncle Ray asked,

"Would you like a puppy?" Jenny stopped. This puppy was it; this was her hoped-for, begged-for, prayed-for dog.

"Yes, we want a puppy, and we'd really like this puppy!" John and James nodded in agreement. All three children tripped over each other and the stairs as they hurried to ask Mom and Dad.

"Mom, Dad, there's a puppy downstairs that we need!" Dad smiled ever so slightly.

"You need a puppy? Or do you want a puppy?" The children could still hear their uncle's muffled broom thudding and yelling from downstairs.

"The puppy needs us, too!" Jenny said breathlessly.

"You'd have to be responsible; we've discussed this before."

"I am very responsible; I care for Johnny and James; I can care for a puppy." Jenny was determined to make her argument. For sure, this was her puppy!

The rest of the day was a blur because all Jenny could think of was the possibility of taking the puppy home. After all, Dad had said, "We'll see," but then they had driven without the puppy back to Grandma and Grandpa's house.

Soon, vacation was over, and the family loaded up the car and headed home. But instead of getting on the main road, heading east and homeward, Dad headed north.

"What are you doing, Paul?"

"I'm going a different way."

"You're going the wrong way." Mom giving Dad directions was the usual topic of conversation during travel. And, for the most part, Dad didn't mind.

"I'll be turning just up here." Dad slowly turned onto the street where Uncle Ray and Aunt Clarine lived.

"Maybe it's time we had a dog. I think Jenny is ready for the responsibility." Jenny couldn't believe it; they were back at Uncle Ray's house, and it could only be for one reason. The puppy was so happy to see them; he wiggled all over as if he understood that he was going to his forever home.

"I'll be first to hold him since I'm the oldest." Jenny took the puppy and held

PACKARD

him close; this was indeed her hoped-for, begged-for, prayed-for puppy. As the thrilled children and puppy traveled home that day, they named him Fritz. After all, the Dachshund breed was of German ancestry.

* * *

The bumpy road and fast descent jolted her from those sweet memories; now, she held

Fritz, her hoped-for, begged-for, prayed-for dog's lifeless body, in her lap.

3 WHAT'S THAT?

At last, the van pulled up to the schoolhouse, which had a small basement apartment serving as the teachers' living quarters. Jenny and Johnny waited for Dad to carefully carry the dog down the stairs into the living room and lay him on the orange Naugahyde couch. The little dog lay still as Dad tried to see if its heart was still beating. Hearing a faint beat, he grabbed the phone and called the local veterinarian.

"You've reached Oroville Animal Hospital. No doctors are on duty today. If it is an emergency, please call the Spokane branch at 516-234-0960." Dad quickly dialed the new number while the children watched breathlessly.

"Hello. You've reached the Spokane Animal Hospital. How may I help you?" Dad quickly told the whole experience.

"We need to get our little dog some antivenom," he stressed.

"I'm sorry, sir; I'm just the answering service. I have no idea if we have any antivenom, and if we did, you would not get here in time." Dad slowly hung up the phone and turned to the children. "I'm sorry, kids, there's nothing we can do." He walked out the door and started unpacking the van. Mom ordered everyone to go out and help him. Soon, all the luggage, sleeping bags, and supplies were piled in the middle of the living room floor. Jenny checked on Fritz, but there was no response.

"Come, Johnny, get James; we'll have a prayer meeting." Soon, they were kneeling behind the school, praying for Fritz. After the last *amen*, she ran inside to check on Fritz, but the dog was still unconscious.

"We're going to pray again. Remember how Naaman had to wash in the river seven times?" The boys looked curiously at Jenny.

"I haven't heard of Naaman, but I don't mind washing in the river."

"How will that help Fritz?" James lisped.

"We're not giving up. We're going to pray seven times," Jenny declared with determination. She pulled the boys down to their knees, and each one prayed for Fritz.

"It's your turn to go and check," Jenny ordered Johnny, who quickly rose and returned to the house to check.

"No, nothing has changed. Mom says he's dead." Johnny announced on his return.

"Let's pray again; this will only be the third time." The children knelt again and bowed their heads.

"Dear Jesus, we prayed for a puppy, and you gave us Fritz. Although it seems hopeless, we believe you can make him well." Jenny hoped God would understand her reasoning.

"James, it's your turn to check."

"I don't want to see a dead dog." James began crying.

"Just go and check," Jenny ordered.

A few minutes later, he returned,

"He's no different; he's just lying there, but his head is bigger than a ball." James took his arms and made a ball shape while he said it.

"Then we'll pray again; it's only been four times." The children begged God to heal their dog.

"It's my turn to check; just wait; I'll be right back." Jenny jumped up and ran into the house. Fritz was still lying on the couch. She ran over to him, gently patting his back, rubbing his tummy, and whispering.

"Fritz, we're talking to God about you." Did she imagine it, or was there a slight tap of his tail on the couch? She ran outside, up the stairs, and back to the waiting boys.

"Pray, pray, pray; it's working; God is healing Fritz! Let's thank Him." The boys dutifully thanked God for making Fritz well, and all three ran back into the house. Sure enough, his tail tapped gently on the couch's surface. Jenny got a cup of water and, taking a teaspoon, dripped water into his mouth. In less than an hour, Fritz started trying to lift his head. It was still the size of a volleyball and looked way out of proportion to the rest of his Dachshund body.

"Try to keep him still," Mom commanded

over her basket of dirty clothes. The children tried, but it was impossible. Fritz raised his head and balanced it precariously on his tiny body. He then jumped off the couch and somersaulted onto the floor. The children squealed with delight, hugging the small dog, and then showed him his food. He ignored it all but went delightedly from child to child, giving doggie kisses with his big head, swollen tongue, and bared teeth. Just then, there was a knock at the door. After knocking, Uncle Art opened the door and peeked his head in.

"What's that?" he exclaimed as Fritz greeted him. Fritz had become adept at balancing his oversized head on his tiny body, and his welcoming wiggle looked strangely counterbalanced. The family all started talking at once; they told Uncle Art about the camping trip, the snake bite, the quick ride home, the hopelessness at not finding any veterinarians or anti-venom, and thinking that Fritz had died.

"Well, it does sound unbelievable, but I'm happy for you. And for your little dog." He patted the small dog's large head and turned his conversation to his challenges with his recently acquired apple orchard.

That night, as Jenny slid in between the sheets of her bed, she thought of the day's events and how tired she was.

"Hey, Jenny, are you asleep?" Johnny asked softly from the bed across the room. "I want to hear what happened to the men who had our mummy bags."

"Aren't you sleepy?" Jenny responded.

"Yes, but I can't sleep; I keep thinking of things." He patted the little dog who lay next to him. Fritz always began the evening at Johnny's bed because James still slept in the crib.

"Well, I think we left off with Ray and Mark seeing the light from the castle."

"Yes, I remember, so then what happened?"

* * *

"The men crawled out of their mummy bags, shook the sand out, rolled them neatly, and tied them to the bottom of their backpacks. The other soldiers slept soundly and didn't notice Mark and Ray quietly leaving the camp. The light continued to flicker the message, and the men hurried toward the castle wall. They murmured about the different possibilities. Both young men had some experience in cliff climbing, and each had a rope in their backpack.

'This will be pretty dangerous since we don't have time to put our safety rope up.' Mark scratched his head; he always did that when he was thinking.

It wasn't long before they arrived at their first obstacle. A 10-foot barbed wire fence with curling razor wire at the top went all the way around the castle except for the side that faced the ocean. Here, the prison fence stopped and connected to a sheer cliff. The waves splashed and crashed against the granite surface.

'We can try and go under the wire, but they may have dogs, and if they bark, that will give us away.' Mark scratched his head again.

'I think we need to go up the cliffside; if we fall, the water might save us.' Ray added."

* * *

"Which way do you want them to go?" Jenny asked Johnny. There was no sound except the tapping of Fritz's feet as he walked over to Jenny's bed. And the soft guitar music from her parents' bedroom. Jenny smiled. *Thank you, Jesus, for my hoped-for, begged-for, prayed-for dog.*

4 Zzzzzzzzip

"Hey, do you own a black Dachshund?" The gruff voice on the other end of the party line asked?

"Yes, we do," Mom answered.

"Well, I thought I'd let you know that he's on the highway chasing cars. Soon, he'll be a pancake."

"Thank you; we'll see if we can get him now." Mom hung up the phone and turned to Jenny.

"Your dog is all the way out on the highway." Jenny froze. What was she to do? The driveway was about a mile long and wound around the orchard and through an alfalfa field. She wasn't even supposed to go down it. As much as she was responsible, how would she ever get Fritz back?

"Come on, we'll take the car and get him."

"Thanks, Dad. I'm sorry I wasn't watching him. We didn't have to worry for a few weeks because his head was so swollen he didn't venture very far."

The two got in the Volkswagen van and headed down the driveway. Sure enough, there he was, just waiting beside the road for the next car to come along.

"Come, Fritz." The dog wagged his tail and ran to Jenny. She scooped him in her arms and climbed into the car.

"You know, we have to teach him a lesson," Dad said.

"I know, but how do we do that?" Jenny held the dog, who gave her a slurpy kiss. *How do you teach a dog not to go down to the road?* Dad drove up the drive; he didn't say anything, and Jenny could tell he was deep in thought. *Was Dad trying to figure out how to teach Fritz not to go down to the main road?*

"Hey, Paul, your brother called, and he needs help picking apples," Mom announced when they arrived home.

This announcement meant that Jenny and Johnny would be on top of tall ladders, and Dad and Uncle Art would move them around while they were perched there. It was pretty terrifying.

"I don't want to pick apples."

"You will pick apples; Uncle Art is paying us, and we need the money."

You didn't argue with Mom. The kids got in the van, and the family began the trek down the long driveway.

"Hey, Fritz is following us!" exclaimed Johnny. Dad stopped the van, got out, and yelled.

"Go home!" Fritz stopped, but as soon as Dad got back in the car, he ran to catch up. Dad stopped the van again, got out, and ran toward the little dog. Shocked at the menacing figure yelling, "Go home," Fritz turned tail and headed for home.

"That should do it," Dad said as he continued down the drive.

"He's coming again; he's running." Fritz was running as fast as his short legs would carry him. Dad slammed on the brakes; the kids slid off the plastic seats, and Mother braced herself against the dashboard. Dad jumped out of the van. And then he unbuckled his belt. Zzzzzzzzzip! That horrible sound of Dad's leather belt sent chills down Jenny's spine.

Oh no, not the belt! Jenny had felt the sting of that belt before. Dad began running toward Fritz. Fritz stopped. *Should I go or come? Does this mean I get to go now?* As Dad reached the dog, he started whipping the belt. First, it hit Fritz's nose, and with a yelp, he turned and began running back home. But Dad didn't stop, yelling, "Stay home," and whipping the dog. Sometimes, the belt hit the rocks, and sometimes Fritz's backside. The dog's yelps and cries were now filling the valley. And Jenny began crying too. Soon, everyone was crying.

"Stop crying now!" Mom ordered. "Fritz has to learn a lesson. Which would you rather? A dead dog or a sad dog. It is for his good." The sobbing stopped, and Jenny, Johnny, and James watched as their dad returned to the van, checking ever so often to see if Fritz was following him. From their vantage point, the children could see the little dog sitting forlornly at the front steps of their basement apartment. Everyone rode silently to Uncle Art's house across the Okanogan River Road Bridge.

"Hi, kids, are you ready to pick some apples?" Uncle Art was the best. He and Auntie Win made sure the kids had treats and things they knew the family could not afford. On the Sundays that they came to pick apples, they always had delicious potato salad and baked beans for supper.

Afterward, everyone would gather around Uncle Art's big TV and watch The Wonderful World of Disney.

In the meantime, Fritz grew tired of waiting. Maybe he'd find another family. Descending the hill, he turned east toward a white farmhouse about a mile from the church school. It was hard to see above the alfalfa, but the adventure would be better than sitting around all day. After that rude treatment, he didn't know if his family would return. A stretch of nicely mowed green grass lay before him as he broke out of the field. Red geraniums bordered the walk. There was a dog dish with some dried food and a watering device; as he drank, the container gurgled, and more water came into the bowl. Then he sensed something or someone looking at him. He turned with a startled yip. The dog was twice his size, black and white—possibly a border collie or shepherd mix.

I see you are helping yourself.

My family has been gone a long time, and I'm lonely on the hill.

Well, you are welcome to hang out with me. My humans call me Tippy because of the white tip on my tail.

After the two dogs explored Tippy's property, Fritz decided he had better be home when his family returned.

When the Dorys arrived back home, Fritz sat there, looking innocent. The kids jumped out and gave him welcoming hugs.

"Good boy, you have learned your lesson."

That evening, as the kids settled into their beds. Johnny had to ask.

"Jenny, are you asleep? Do you want to tell me more of the story about our mummy bags?"

"Sure," Jenny replied as softly as possible. She could hear Dad's guitar playing, so she knew she could get some of the story told before Mom stopped them.

* * *

"Mark and Ray decided to scale up the cliff on the waterside. The big rocks and stones making up the castle's wall would give them footholds.

'Do you think we have enough rope? And what is our plan when we get to the top?' Mark looked at Ray,

'I don't know what to expect. We'll just have to try.'

'We may die trying.'"

* * *

"Jenny, when are you going to put a horse in the story?"

"Soon, now be quiet and listen."

* * *

"Ray began hiding the guns, knives, and K-rations under a bush.

'Don't tell me we aren't taking any weapons.'

'We aren't taking any weapons?' There was a slight pause. 'We can't possibly haul all the gear to the top. We'll have to rely on God's miracle for this one.' The men silently finished their task, erased their tracks, and then headed toward the waterside of the castle.

Perched high above the rocks and cliffs, they could see one row of windows.

'Keep an eye on the window from which the SOS signal light came; that is where we will head.'

Soon, their eyes were accustomed to the darkness, and their ears seemed to take on sonar qualities."

* * *

"Jenny, what does *accustomed* mean?"

"It means *get used to.*"

"I'm getting tired, Jenny. I hope a horse comes soon." Jenny stopped her story. She could hear her dad playing his guitar and singing the song *Have I Told You Lately That I Love You?*

"Fritz, here, Fritz," Jenny whispered. The dog moved from Johnny's bedside and came over to Jenny's rug. She put her hand down and held his soft ear. That was the last thing she remembered until morning.

"Hi, Mama. Have you seen Fritz?

"I let him out around 5:00 am." Mom continued putting the oatmeal and milk in the bowls. She put one teaspoon of brown sugar on top, along with half of a banana. It was a treat to get the banana and brown sugar; sometimes, all they had to eat was the oatmeal. Jenny went to the door.

"Fritz, Fritz, where are you?" She looked outside, but there was no sign of the dog.

"Jenny, come back and eat your breakfast." The family gathered around the table, and Dad said grace.

"And bring Fritz back safely," Jenny added.

"I'm sure Fritz will return by the time school begins," Dad reassured her. That was the nice thing about living under the school;

you could see your dog at recess, and he could even come to class.

School began, and Jenny looked out the window; she still hadn't seen Fritz.

"Stay at your desk." Mrs. Dory ordered. Jenny thought about explaining why she had gone to the window, but then decided against it. At recess, Jenny, Johnny, James, and their school friends climbed the hills; they looked under the sagebrush and in their tumbleweed forts. All the time, calling at the top of their lungs. "Fritz! Fritz! Fritz!"

It was almost impossible to eat supper and even more impossible to go to sleep. Jenny's voice was hoarse, and she didn't feel like telling a story. She looked at the empty rag rugs and felt sick.

5 The Pit

Smells good. Fritz followed the scent up the hill. The delicious smell grew stronger. *Smells like good food.* By now, Fritz was pressing his nose against the wooden boards of the garbage pit cover. He strained every muscle to get closer to the food. And then the cover gave way, and down, down Fritz plummeted. Startled, he lay still and then started eating supper's leftovers. His landing had been soft and spongy, and being so close to so much food was splendid. He ran around the pit, eating every scrap he could find. When the scraps were gone, he began digging and unearthing all kinds of odiferous delicacies.

This is a great spot. Fritz thought, "There's plenty of food, good digging, and a *nice soft bed for sleeping."* Fritz didn't plan to share it with his human family or Tippy. When he heard the kids calling his name, he munched on a carrot and took a nap.

In the meantime, Jenny began the second school day without Fritz. At every recess, the children called for Fritz but heard nothing. Even Mom and Dad started to fear the worst.

"Kids, we will all look for Fritz this evening after supper. So, eat well; we're going hiking." Dad's announcement brought some relief, and the kids found their appetite. The kids ate their meal of beans and rice and urged their parents to hurry and finish.

"I've watched you and your school friends look everywhere around the school and play area, but we are going to take another look; Fritz may be hurt and can't bark." Dad led them up the hill on the north side of the property and had each person spread out.

"We'll walk slowly and keep calling. Use these sticks to beat the bushes." Dad was on one end, and Johnny, Jenny, James, and Mom were on the other. There was six feet between each person, making a search grid of about 30 feet. Carefully, they went over the hilly portion of the play area, looking under sagebrush and in their tumbleweed forts. At 300 ft, they arrived at the school building and searched around the window wells, bushes, and burn barrel. After exploring that side of the property, they began the same process on the other side. After another thirty feet, they ascended to the top of the south side of the property and the garbage pit. Fritz heard them coming. His life in the pit had been fantastic at first, but a dog could only dig so much, and the best food scraps were gone.

"Fritz, Fritz, FRITZ!" He could hear his name.

"Ruff, ruff, " he responded. But they kept calling: "Fritz, Fritz, FRITZ!" There was a thumping above him as Johnny and James began playing King of the Mountain on top of the garbage pit lid.

"Stop jumping; it could break, and you'd get hurt, " scolded Mom. The thumping stopped, and Fritz noticed the light dimming as the whole family sat down to rest and lay back

on the garbage pit cover. *Surely, they must know I am down here.* Fritz began wagging his tail. He could hear the kids' voices as they spotted shapes in the clouds. *Ruff, Ruff,* the voices stopped.

"Did you hear that?" No one moved.

"Ruff, Ruff!"

"I can hear Fritz!"

"Fritz, Fritz." The family jumped up from the pit cover.

"Stand back; I don't want anyone to fall in." Dad pushed the cover back and peered over the edge.

"Yes, he's down there. And now we have to figure out how to get him out."

Earlier that spring, Dad and some friends borrowed an extra-long ladder and dug the garbage pit bucket-full by bucket-full, but Dad had returned the ladder to its owner.

Dad's ladders weren't long enough to reach the full extent of the pit; he had an eight-foot stepladder and another eight-foot single ladder. Opening the stepladder, Dad let it slide down the side, hoping it would miss Fritz.

Thankfully, the stepladder landed upright and close to the side of the pit. Next, Dad, lying on his stomach and sliding the single ladder down the side of the pit, saw that the single ladder didn't quite reach the stepladder below.

"Jenny, can you make it down this ladder while I hold it and get Fritz?" Jenny peered over the side. She felt her stomach churn. Dad was holding the ladder, but it wasn't touching anything at the bottom.

"I don't think I can do it." Jenny began to cry.

"Stop crying!" Mother demanded.

"Come here, son, you can do this." Johnny, much smaller than Jenny, climbed over his father's head, got on the single ladder, and quickly descended it. By now, everyone was lying on their stomachs and looking over the edge.

As Johnny reached the stepladder, he hesitated.

"Hang on tight to this ladder." Dad jiggled the single ladder ever so slightly. "And make sure you have a firm footing on the stepladder." The wobbly stepladder settled under Johnny's weight. And soon, Johnny was getting his face licked and holding a happy Fritz. *Now, I have a dog and my son in the garbage pit*, thought Dad.

"Get a good hold of Fritz with one arm and climb back out," Dad instructed.

Everyone held their breath. Johnny was only five years old, and Fritz, as little as he was, was still pretty heavy. The little boy grasped the dog tightly around the middle and started climbing up the stepladder. Once Johnny reached the single ladder, the task became almost impossible. Dad decided to tie a rope around the first rung to get more length. Using Mom, Jenny, and James as anchors, he used his arms to extend the single ladder and reach the stepladder.

"Come on, son, you can do it." Fritz wiggled, and Johnny almost lost him.

"See if you can get one of your feet up to the first rung and then use that to help you get onto the ladder." Johnny struggled but finally got Fritz and himself onto the single ladder. Dad's muscles flexed and bulged as he began to pull the ladder up. The rest of the family pulled on the rope behind him, keeping it taut.

"You're doing well, son. Don't let go." When the ladder was high enough, Dad gently brought it parallel to the pit opening and pulled it toward him. He grasped Johnny and Fritz. Free from the pit, Fritz ran from child to child, barking and wiggling all over.

"We'd better get back home before it gets dark." Dad pulled the lid over the pit and placed large rocks on it. A sliver of orange was still glowing in the west, making the faraway mountain range appear black as the family descended the hill and into the safety of their basement apartment. No one complained about having to go to bed that night.

Everything seems back in balance, thought Jenny, looking at Fritz sitting by

James's crib. The toddler reached his hands between the crib bars and lovingly touched the dog.

"Jenny, tell the story," Johnny ordered in a hoarse whisper.

"OK."

* * *

"The granite sides of the castle allowed Ray and Mark to climb it like rock climbers, and soon, they were looking into a small, unlit cell.

'Psst, is anyone here?' someone responded in a language they didn't understand.

'Americans?' Mark asked. Someone came to the barred opening and motioned to the right. The two soldiers edged their way to the next window opening. This opening did not have bars and looked like it led to a hall.

The men carefully let themselves down over the sill. They were in the castle! Pausing for a minute to figure out where they were and where the light had been, they carefully began working through the hallways, hiding behind pillars and statues whenever a guard came by."

* * *

Fritz moved from James's crib to Johnny's bed. Jenny paused in her storytelling.

"I want a horse in the story," Johnny said, fighting his drowsiness. That was the last thing Johnny said, and then Fritz moved to Jenny's bed. Somehow, Fritz always knew when the kids went to sleep. While stroking Fritz's head, she thought long and hard about how she could incorporate a horse into her story.

6 The Spark

"Time to get up in the morning when the birds begin to sing," Jenny woke up with a start to her mom's singing.

"Where is Fritz?"

"He's right here," Dad said, pointing down to the little dog waiting patiently for breakfast food scraps.

Mom looked the other way that morning while the kids dropped bread and banana slices for Fritz. It was going to be a great day at school.

After breakfast, the kids ran up the back stairs past their dad, who was filling the boiler with sawdust. The fall air was chilly, and the school upstairs needed some heat. Mom followed close behind the kids; when Mom and Dad went up the stairs to the school, they became Mr. and Mrs. Dory instead of Mom and Dad.

After getting the boiler going, Dad would get in the VW van and pick up students from Tonasket and Orville. Jenny watched out the window for the bus while Johnny and James decided what toys to have under the large reading table. They were too young for school, so their lives consisted of playing quietly under the table and going out at recess with the school kids. Even though Fritz was free to roam the room, he spent most of his time under the table, too.

"The bus, the bus is here!" Jenny was so excited to tell her friends about Fritz. "Emma May, Fritz is back!" Emma May was a cute, chubby little girl. Her father was a sheep herder, and everyone said he was 90. Emma May sat down on the floor and welcomed

Fritz with outstretched arms. The dog licked her face while she giggled.

"Where did you find him?" Emma May asked. Jenny could hardly wait to tell the whole story, including how they finally got the ladders back out after getting Fritz out.

"I'm so glad he's back." Soon, the bus with Hughie and Danny arrived; they were just as excited as Emma May to see the little dog back in the schoolhouse.

At recess, the schoolchildren ran to their various Tumbleweed forts. The school was so new that it didn't have any playground equipment or even one ball. The sagebrush and tumbleweeds were their play equipment and Jenny's imagination. Soon, all the kids were playing cowboys and Indians, and Johnny galloped all over the hillside on his "horse." Fritz was a wolf, and James was a dog, who happily crawled on all fours and barked.

Besides recess, the next best part of the day was room duties. And the best room duty was any duty where you had to go outside. This week, Jenny and Emma May had Trash Duty.

"I'll carry the trash cans, and you can dump the papers in." Jenny and Emma went from their classroom to the big kids' room (grades 5-8), smooshing the papers into one can. Once outside, they had to be careful that the wind didn't catch the paper trash before getting it into the burn barrel.

"Let's crumple the paper into snowballs and see if we can get them into the barrel." Jenny was already forming a ball as she spoke. Emma May followed her example. The game was fun; soon, the barrel was full of snowballs.

Whoosh, with a gust of wind, the balls of paper ignited. The two little girls stood in wonderment.

"Wow! Did you see that?" Emma May nodded her head but seemed speechless. Jenny slowly bent down into their wastebasket and picked up another piece of paper. Then, ever so slowly, she began crumpling it into a ball while keeping her eyes on the flames. Then she threw it into the burn barrel. Both girls were amazed when it, too, began to burn. Now, every piece of

paper became an amazing visual display, and the girls were sad when the last page was gone.

"We need to stir it; let's find some sticks." Jenny had seen Dad stir the burn barrel before. Both girls started sticking their sticks into the fire and watched in amazement as pieces of paper ash, glowing around the edges, floated effortlessly into the wind.

"Waah!" cried Emma May. Jenny grabbed her away from the falling embers.

"I can't see any fire on you." Jenny carefully inspected Emma May's arms, head, and legs.

"It's not my arm, it is my dress." Emma May sobbed inconsolably while showing Jenny the hole in her dress.

"It's the only school dress I have, " she continued to cry. Now Jenny was crying, too.

Would this mean her friend couldn't come to school? The rule was that you had to wear a dress. Jenny had three school dresses. She wore a different dress on Monday, Tuesday, and Wednesday, then repeated the pattern on Thursday and Friday. But Emma May wore the same dress every day. Leaving the burn barrel, the two girls solemnly returned to the school.

"Emma May burned her dress, and she has no more dresses." Mrs. Dory looked at the two girls. Clean lines of tears streaked down their soot-smudged faces. Mrs. Dory carefully examined the dress and only found one small hole.

"She can have one of my dresses," offered Jenny

"Then go downstairs and get your two dresses hanging in the closet. We'll see which one Emma May likes." Both girls brighten at the idea. And Jenny returned with the dresses.

"I like the pink checkered one." Emma May touched the dress reverently. "I will look beautiful in it, just like you, Jenny."

"You can go and change into it now, and I'll take the burned dress and fix it so you will have two dresses." That evening, Mom got out the sewing machine and carefully undid part of the gathered waistline. Then, she took a small seam the length of the skirt that encompassed the hole. Then she gathered the material and sewed it back to the bodice.

"That looks perfect." Jenny admired her mother's sewing work.

"Emma May will now have two school dresses, and so will I."

Soon it was bedtime, and everyone in the

Dory family went to bed at the same time.

"Hey, Johnny, do you want to hear more of the story?"

"Yeah, if it has a horse in it."

"The horses come into the story tonight," Jenny assured him. With that announcement, Johnny lifted himself on one elbow and listened intently.

* * *

"After Mark and Ray had searched six rooms, they came to the room holding the Americans. They pulled a 15-inch pry bar from their backpack, and without saying a word, they began working on the door. Surprisingly, the door opened silently. The prisoners were thin and covered in dried blood. Motioning to follow, they quietly left their cell and followed Mark and Ray out of the room down the hall; along the way, Mark silently pried other cell doors open until they had a rather large following. Everyone climbed over the windowsill and onto the ground.

'Come quickly; horses are at the back of the castle.' Ray and Mark followed the man, who led them around the castle to the stables. The horses neighed softly and seemed to understand that they were part of an important plan."

* * *

"Hey, Johnny, see, I told you there'd be horses in the story." There was no response. Fritz moved from Johnny's to Jenny's rug.

7 The Peanut

Jenny woke up with a start; it was so quiet. Johnny was still sleeping, so she carefully got on his bed to peer out the basement window, but she couldn't see a thing. Letting herself land with a little bounce, she stared at her brother.

"What do you want?" he asked sleepily

"First, did you hear about the horses in last night's story?"

"Yes, and I want to know which one Mark is riding."

"Never mind that. I can't see out the window." Now Johnny was curious. They could always see out their window; it looked right onto the ground and up the hill at their tumbleweed forts. Now, both children stood

on Johnny's bed and looked out the window.
All they could see was white.

"That's pretty strange. I wonder where
everything went?"

"Time for breakfast!" Tripping over each
other, they competed to tell Mom about the
window. Then they ran to the front door,
where they'd have a better view.

"Don't open the door! I've put Fritz out,
and I don't want him to return until he's done
his business." Jenny and Johnny peered out
the window. James wanted to see, too, but
he wasn't tall enough, so Jenny lifted him.
Everything was white except the outside wall
that faced the door, and even that had white
along the edges of the brick. Beyond the
brick stairwell, they could see Fritz
delightedly jumping and hopping in the snow.

"He's having fun without us!" Johnny grudgingly exclaimed.

After breakfast, Mom began to bundle everyone up. Jenny got her coat, the one Mom had made with scraps of wool from many coats. The sleeves were white from one of Mom's coats, the front of the coat was red from one of Grandma's coats, the back was tweed from a wool suit coat of Dad's, and the hood was black and white checkered; everyone called it the coat of many coats. Soon, all three children were layered in sweaters, coats, socks, mittens, and plastic bread bags over their shoes for boots.

"Open the door slowly," cautioned Mom. As they did, light fluffy snow spilled into the room, along with a happy dog.

"Come, Fritz, yougettogo. We all get to go!" They began to climb the steps up to the yard.

"Jenny, help!" She looked back and saw that James had slid back down the steps. As she went to help, she lost her footing, too.

"Johnny, help us!" Johnny stood at the top of the steps and smiled mischievously. This wonderland was terrific, and he hated returning down the slippery steps. Jenny figured out she would have more traction if she came up the stairs on her knees. Knee by knee, she pulled herself and James up to the top. Once out in the yard, they all began exploring. The snowstorm had blown the roofs off their tumbleweed forts, but that meant that the floors had nice snow, too; the challenge was getting the snow-laden tumbleweeds balanced again on top.

"Now we can stamp out designs and make rooms." Soon, they were lost in their imaginative world of castles, soldiers, and horses.

"Time to come in!" Mom's loud voice brought them out of their play and quickly returned them to reality. Looking at the top of the steps, they were relieved that Dad had cleared the snow so it wouldn't be so challenging to get into the apartment. Once inside, Mom began peeling off their clothes.

Their hands, faces, and feet were red, and everything was wet.

"You should see it out there. Everything is white, and we fixed up our forts. It is amazing! Can we go out again after lunch?"

"You can't go out until your clothes have dried." And that was that. But it didn't deter the joyous retelling of the morning's snowy adventure.

After lunch, Johnny got out his tricycle; he had gotten it for his birthday. It was the best birthday present anyone in the family had ever gotten. It was shiny red with white trim and a chrome fender. There was a place where someone could stand on the back, and Johnny would often give rides. Around and around the living area, he would zoom. Mom was cleaning the fridge; Dad

was working on some schoolwork. Jenny and James waited by the door on the other end of the living room where Johnny would stop to pick up a passenger, but today, with that impish grin, he kept riding by. James had had enough of the teasing and chased after the speeding tricycle. As he ran, he spotted a few peanuts among the refrigerator items on the table and paused to grab some. Johnny took the opportunity to speed even faster. James grabbed the back of Johnny's shirt and tried to get a foot on the tricycle's back platform. He screamed in frustration; it all happened on the inhale. The peanuts had gone down the wrong pipe!

Dad sprang from his chair and swung James upside down, whacking him on the back—out shot peanuts, pinging across the floor. The little boy turned blue; Dad whacked some more, and out came one more peanut. Dad opened James's mouth to see if he could see anything, but it looked clear. Tears were streaming down James's face, but no crying sounds were coming out. Dad tried again, and at last, James emitted a thin, high whistle that could be heard on a long inhale, and another lower whistle sound that could be heard on the exhale. Everyone watched as the littlest member of the family struggled for breath.

"Jenny, grab your coat and take Fritz out. Johnny, put your trike away. Paul, take James to the car. We are going to the hospital." Everyone did what Mom ordered robotically.

"Sorry, you don't get to go," Jenny whispered to Fritz as she made sure he had food and water. Then, she quietly went and

got in the VW van with the rest of the family.
Mom held James in the front seat while Dad
drove. No one spoke, and in less than 10
minutes, they arrived at the Oroville
Community Hospital. The hospital had just
been completed the year before, in 1962,
and the highly polished terrazzo floors felt
cold and sterile. Dad carried James to a blue
Naugahyde-covered chair while Mom went
to the counter and explained the situation.

"Mr. and Mrs. Dory, the doctor will see
you now."

"Jenny, take care of Johnny." And then
they were gone. Jenny looked at Johnny;
she wanted to cry, scream, or run after them,
but she had to be brave; she had to take
care of Johnny.

"Johnny, let's get under the chairs." They
both got under a chair, side by side, and

looked at each other through the wooden braces.

"Are you going to tell me a story?" Johnny looked into Jenny's eyes.

"Your eyes have speckles of gold in them. Did you know that, Jenny?"

"Your eyes don't have any speckles of gold; they are just pure blue." It's funny that Jenny hadn't noticed that about Johnny's eyes before.

"You have piercing blue eyes, Johnny."

"I hope *piercing* is a good word."

"Yes, it just means to poke through something."

"I have poking blue eyes! That sounds dumb."

"Never mind about your eyes; as long as you can see with them, they're good."

"OK, story time." Johnny leaned back against the rail. *He thought that if Jenny could tell a story, then everything would be OK.* Jenny adjusted herself in the cramped space and spoke in a whisper.

* * *

"Mark and Ray motioned to each other to untie all the horses' ropes. They took the saddles that were lined up on the corral fence and began getting the horses ready. Ray had just picked out a spirited black stallion when suddenly, they heard a shout, the lights came on, and a siren went off.

'Forget the saddles; every man for himself!' Mark opened the corral gate and swung up on a palomino. Other men on horses and riderless horses began stampeding out of the corral. They galloped into the night, and the sounds of hooves spread across the countryside.

'Ray, Ray!' yelled Mark in a hoarse whisper.

'Hey Buddy, I'm right here behind you. I figured the best way to stay together was to follow the white of your horse.' Both men pulled their horses to a walk."

* * *

"Hey, Jenny, thanks for giving me a palomino. But why does Mark have to sound like a horse? Can't he be human?

"What are you talking about? Of course, Mark is human."

"But you said, 'horse whisper'."

"That just means his throat was scratchy when he talked." Johnny leaned back against the chair brace.

* * *

"The men and horses were now walking along the edge of the field in the shadows of the trees.

'Where do you think we are?'

'I have no idea. But let's continue in the opposite direction from the castle.'

'Yes, and we have pretty much lost all of our supplies. We don't even know the fate of the other Americans.' The two men continued in silence; feeling exhausted, they would try to take a nap while riding their horses."

* * *

"Jenny, how do you sleep while riding on a horse?"

"Let's shut our eyes and pretend we're sleeping on a horse." Both children shut their eyes and rocked back and forth on their pretend horses.

"Get up!" The sharp words from Mom immediately brought them out of their make-believe.

"How is he? Did they get the peanut out?" But Jenny knew the answer. James was still lifelessly draped across Dad's arms. And Mom's face was etched with stress.

"We must take James to Spokane; they can't help him here." The ride home was quiet, except for the painful whistling of James struggling for each breath.

8 The Man

"I want you to hold James for a while. We must pack, arrange substitute teachers, and find someone to care for you and Johnny." Jenny climbed up on the couch, and her mom placed the semiconscious toddler in her lap. She put her hand under his tiny hand. She had always been fascinated by his hands.

* * *

When James was born, Jenny was four years old. The family lived in a big two-bedroom log cabin in Idaho. Grandpa Dory had one bedroom, and in the other bedroom, there was one big bed for Mom and Dad. Along the outside wall were two small cots, one for Jenny and one for Johnny. Both bedrooms opened into a large living room. In the kitchen, a wood-burning cook stove, kept the whole house warm.

When Mom and Dad told the kids about the new addition to the family, it was a happy announcement. Now Jenny understood why Mom would spend her evenings embroidering baby gowns—she called it a layette. Mom had broken her ankle at the beginning of winter while sliding down the hill behind the cabin. Now, she hobbled with crutches while Dad taught in town at the public school.

"Pst, time to get up; we don't want to wake Grandpa." Jenny and Johnny wore their coats over their pajamas and obediently followed Dad to the car. Mom was already in the front seat, moaning softly.

"Where are we going?" Johnny asked.

"How can you ask a question like that?"

"I just wanted to make sure."

"We're going to Fairfield (Washington), where Mom's doctor, Dr. Hart, is." Once they arrived at the Fairfield clinic, Dad dropped Jenny and Johnny off at Uncle Art and Auntie Win's house.

"Be good. Soon, we'll be back with a baby." Auntie Win had a big house, and all the cousins came over the next day. They bounced on the trampoline and played hide-and-seek, running all over the three-story home. Jenny was introduced to her new baby brother, James, three days later. All she wanted to do was hold and touch the beautiful baby boy.

"Go play, leave that baby alone." Mom would scold.

Once they returned home and entered their routine, Jenny found ways to help.

"Jenny, can you go and check on James? He's sleeping on my bed." Jenny went into the bedroom, and in the middle of Mom and Dad's bed lay James, swaddled up and sound asleep. Jenny got on the bed and began rolling him over to the edge. Once he was close to the edge of the bed, she got on the floor, gave him a little push, and then caught him in her arms.

"Look, Mommy. Here is James. I caught him when he was about to roll off your bed." Jenny brought the baby to Mom.

"Thank you, dear. Can you get me some diapers?"

"Can I change his diaper?"

"No, that is one task you are still too little to do."

* * *

How can something as small as a peanut possibly do this to James? Jenny felt a lump in her throat and tears in her eyes.

Once Auntie Win arrived, Mom, Dad, and James headed for Spokane. The hospital had been alerted that a little boy who had inhaled a peanut was arriving. And they immediately ushered them into an examination room. The doctor listened to James's chest and frowned.

"This is a grave situation. We just had a ten-year-old girl in here who had inhaled a peanut." Then, the doctor was silent.

"Yes, and how did that turn out?" Dad asked.

"It didn't turn out very well." Mom and Dad just looked at each other. The doctor continued speaking as if what he had just told them was an everyday occurrence.

"We will perform a bronchoscopy by inserting a tube with a camera down his lungs and see where the foreign object is. You are fortunate because our bronchoscope is a recently acquired technology, something we could not have done last year."

"Here are the papers to sign." The admitting officer gave them a stack of papers.

"Nurse, take him to surgery." James looked like a small white lump in the big hospital bed. Both parents kissed him, and then he was rolled away.

"I feel so helpless!" Dad put his face in

his hands and wept; Mother patted him on the back, her face lined with worry.

In the surgical unit, they prepped for the procedure. Spraying some local anesthetic on the tube, the doctor slowly inserted it into James's lung. The plan was to place a small amount of sterile water through the scope and then suck the peanut up with the water. All the while, James was still laboriously breathing on his own. Down went the tube, exploring each lobe (three lobes in the right lung and two in the left lung).

"There it is, I see it, just one peanut half."

"Can you reach it?"

"Water, please." The surgical nurse followed the doctor's orders and inserted sterile water into the tube.

"I can't reach it on the inhale because it lies flat. But I'm hoping I can reach in on the exhale. I can see it standing up on end. But it is vibrating and slippery." The doctor tried for more than an hour to get the peanut. James's blood pressure increased, and his heart began to beat rapidly.

"We'd better stop; we are doing more harm than good." The doctor moved away from the operating table, removed his gloves, and wiped the perspiration from his face.

"I'll go talk to the parents. You can finish up here. Make sure to put him in an oxygen tent." The doctor said as he left the operating room, walked down the hall, and through the swinging doors into the emergency waiting room. As he went up to the Dorys, he averted his gaze. There was no smile or words of assurance—just an explanation.

"We tried, but the peanut is just out of

reach of our bronchoscope."

"No, no, that can't be. He's just a little boy. I'm sure your bronchoscope is more than long enough."

"We could touch the peanut, but it was too slippery to grab, and we had to stop trying. Tomorrow, we can remove it surgically, but it comes with a lot of risk. Your son will then have to be intubated."

"When can we see him?"

"We are setting him up in an oxygen tent now. I'll send a nurse down as soon as he is situated. If you are praying, people, now is the time to pray. I can't give you false hope; this situation is serious." Then the doctor turned on his heel and was gone.

Shortly, a nurse appeared and informed them that they could see James. Over the top of his bed was a large, clear plastic tent.

He remained unconscious and didn't respond to any of their questions. The heartbroken and weary parents left the room and headed out to the parking lot. Only then did they realize that they would have to spend the night in the car. They couldn't drive the four hours back home and come again in the morning.

"Hi, Paul and Melba." Startled, they looked to see who was calling their names.

"Your pastor called me and said you were here in Spokane with your son."

"Yes, Mr. Perry, he has been admitted to the hospital. It is a serious situation." Dad tried to sound unemotional, but his fear was evident.

"We have the state-wide prayer warriors praying for your son. It is in God's hands." Mr. Perry, their Educational Superintendent, put his hand on Dad's shoulder.

"Yes, it is in God's hands," Dad repeated. But how could he make those words his own? He didn't want his son to die.

"I've come to take you to my home. We have a guest room prepared for you." Mom and Dad looked at each other, then followed him in a daze.

During the early hours of the night, James regained consciousness. *Where am I? What is that funny sound?* He played around with the whistling of the peanut, discovering that he could control the frequency and pitch. He looked carefully at the tent; the oxygen concentrator hummed on the floor beside his bed. He tapped the plastic; he wanted to cry, but was too tired. At some point, a nurse came in and changed his diaper. He was upset to discover he was wearing a diaper, but she said it was only for one night. He was also hungry, but could not have any food since he was scheduled to have surgery in the morning. Instead, she gave him a good-tasting pill, and then he didn't remember anything until about 4:00 am.

A bright light filled his room, and a tall man entered and walked over to his bed. The man lifted the plastic and leaned close to James. James didn't feel afraid; in fact, he felt happy.

"When the doctor comes to see you in the morning, please tell him to hold you upside down and pat you on the back; you will be able to cough the peanut up." James's eyes were wide with wonder, and he nodded in understanding.

"But why can't you hold me? I'll cough

really hard for you."

"It is for the doctor's benefit." Then the man was gone. James fell back asleep and awoke to a magical world of sparkling diamonds and prisms as the sun shone through his oxygen tent. And then the doctor entered.

"Good morning, Little Man. How are you today?" Not expecting an answer, the doctor was surprised when James began to talk.

"A man came into my room last night and told me that you should hold me upside down, and I should cough hard, and you should hit me on the back." With a puzzled look, the doctor picked James up from the bed and held him upside down.

"Are you ready?"

"Yes, I'm ready, and I'm going to cough hard," James struggled to talk.

Without any more discussion, the doctor held him upside down and gave a good whack on James's back; James coughed and out shot the peanut.

James smiled. The doctor gently put him back in bed and retrieved the peanut from the tiled floor.

"This is a special peanut, and I want your parents to have it."

Meanwhile, Jenny and Johnny tried to enjoy their stay at Auntie Win and Uncle Art's home. The day had been good, with all the cousins playing and exploring the orchard. But the tears began to flow once night came, and it was just Jenny and Johnny in a big, strange room. Even Fritz had been left behind.

"Jenny, if you tell me a story, you might stop crying."

"I'll t-r-y," she sobbed.

* * *

"Mark and Ray were slumped over their horses, sleeping. When shots rang through the air, they slid off their horses and pressed deep into the bushes. Were the shots directed at them? They held perfectly still, and the horses remained calm. Then, they saw the troop of soldiers mounted on motorcycles coming toward them. Should they try to outrun them? Mark motioned for them to remain still. And sure enough, the brigade roared right past.

'Why did they shoot?'

'Just to scare us and hope we'd reveal ourselves in our fright.'

'They almost succeeded.' Both men were wide awake by now and continued their journey, making sure they were in the shadows of the trees."

9 The Field Trip

"I think it is a good time to take the upper graders on a field trip."

"Yes, Paul, I think you're right. So, what are you thinking?"

"We could go up the mountain and look for wildflowers; it could be part of their science class."

"Could you take Johnny? He gets so tired of always being under the reading table."

"Sure, I'll take Johnny but not James; I imagine we'll climb up some rough terrain."

Dad sent permission slips home with the students that very day. By Friday, everyone in grades 5 – 8 had permission to go on Monday's field trip.

"Yougettogo! Yougettogo!" At the sound

of those jumbled words, Fritz wiggled with joy. He and Johnny would be going on the field trip.

It was a beautiful spring day in the Okanogan Valley, and the students arrived ready for their adventure. After a few instructions, making sure everyone had their lunches and prayer, they followed Mr. Dory out the school doors and into the clear air. They quickly began their climb up the highlands. This small subrange of the Cascade Range was perfect for the novice climber. Those who wanted more of a challenge could scale large boulders, and those less adventurous could quickly move around them. The blue lupines and yellow arrowleafs splashed color among the sagebrush and tumbleweeds. Soon, the group was high enough to look over the entire valley.

"I see the Okanogan River."

"I see Tooley's orchard."

"There's the bridge we cross."

"I see the school; look, the lower grades are going out for recess."

"Hi, everyone, we're up here." Everyone yelled.

"Students, that is enough; look at this lady slipper." Mr. Dory pointed out an interesting-looking flower. "Native American legend says this flower is like a person's journey through life. I suppose it is because it can thrive in such a harsh environment."

The students resumed their climb, and soon it was time for lunch. As they found places to sit, Fritz ran from student to student, happy to have them all down at his level and enjoying the tidbits they gave him.

Johnny found a nice spot under a sagebrush bush. Looking inside his paper bag, he decided to eat his sandwich first.

"Here, Fritz, here Fritz."

Johnny held out a piece of cheese sandwich, one of Fritz's favorites. But since other students were also offering bits of their lunch, he took his time getting to Johnny. Finally, the dog turned around, Johnny was still holding out the cheese sandwich piece and eating the rest with the other hand.

"Grrrrrrrrrrrrrrrrrrr."

"Come on, boy." Johnny waved the piece of food.

"Grrrrrrrrrrrrrrrrrrrrr," The hair on the back of Fritz's neck stood straight up, and he did not move.

"Hey, Dad, I mean Mr. Dory Something is wrong with Fritz; he won't come to me and eat his food. Instead, he's growling at me and looks funny."

Mr. Dory rose from his spot, walked over to Johnny, and then froze.

"Johnny, I want you to do exactly as I say. And don't move a muscle," Dad softly said. "You will slowly reach up with both hands and get a hold of my arm. Keep your body in the same crisscross apple-sauce shape that you are in now, and as I lift you, stay frozen like a statue, don't let your legs down." Johnny slowly raised his arms and grasped Dad's forearm.

"Are you ready, son? It won't be a soft landing." With the speed of lightning, Dad raised Johnny straight up from his place and threw him a few feet away. Startled, Johnny almost began to cry, but remembered that he was with the big kids.

"Look, Fritz likes me again." Fritz was nuzzling him, trying to cheer him up.

"Good job, Johnny!" Mr. Dory gave him a pat on his back as they both watched the big rattlesnake slither back into the crevice of the rock.

"I had wondered why it was such a comfortable place to sit," Johnny said. By now, all the students were looking around to make sure they weren't sitting on a rattlesnake.

"Now that we've finished lunch, we will travel on and keep a watchful eye."

"Daddy, I mean Mr. Dory, which eye is my watchful eye, this one or that one?" Johnny pointed to each eye.

"You need to have watchful eyes!" Dad said, emphasizing the "s." All the students traveled on making sure to watch their steps.

Mom, Jenny, and James listened in amazement to the story that evening.

"I'm thankful that we can all be together, and I believe that Fritz saved you from a

painful bite. I guess he is worth something." Dad, who had never been a little dog fan, patted Fritz's head affectionately.

"Everyone is taking a bath tonight." Mom's announcement received mixed reviews. The apartment bathroom still had no shower, so Mom went to the furnace room. "I have a surprise: Someone gave us another wash tub, so there are two out there ready to go."

"Paul, let's draw straws. A short straw washes kids, and a long straw washes dishes." Dad smiled, cut a straw into two uneven pieces, and handed them to Jenny. She held them in her hand so they looked the same length, and then she had Mom pick.

"Yay, I got the short straw." Mom beckoned the kids to follow her. In the furnace room, there was a table with two metal wash tubs. Each tub had warm water and foamy bubbles. The children used a chair to climb up and get into the tubs.

"I think we can fit James in with Johnny." Mom lifted James into Johnny's tub and began to sing, "Rub-a-dub, dub, three kids in tubs. " Then she handed each kid a clean washcloth and left the room, saying. "Call me if you need me; I'll be helping Dad finish the dishes." Mom closed the door behind her.

"Hey, Jenny, could you tell your story right now?" Johnny asked as he flung some water and bubbles against the sawdust-burning furnace. The bubbles instantly sizzled and vanished. James exuberantly followed suit.

"You'd better stop, or I'm going to tell Mom."

"Then tell us a story."

"I have a better idea. I'm a radio, and these are the radio buttons. One of the buttons tells stories." Jenny held her hands so Johnny could reach the ten buttons." He pressed her thumb first.

"Jesus loves me, this I know . . ." she sang in her most beautiful voice. Johnny quickly pressed another button."

"It will be 70 degrees with a slight chance of thunderstorms..." she announced in her meteorological voice. Johnny quickly changed to another "channel."

"Once upon a time, there were three little pigs . . ."

"Oh, I've heard that story before." Johnny switched channels rapidly, and the kids giggled and argued about what was on each channel. Jenny wanted Johnny to stay on the singing channel, but Johnny wanted the story channel.

All too soon, bath time was over, and they were in their pajamas, all snuggled in their cozy beds. Fritz jumped onto the foot of Jenny's bed and hopped over the crib rail into James's bed. Ever since James had gotten pneumonia, the crib rails had been left down. James turned on his side and put his arm over the dog.

"Now you can tell the story." Whispered Johnny.

"Do you remember everything from before?"

"Yes, they are waiting for the sun to go down so they can go to the barn. Now, go!"

* * *

"Ray woke from his nap just as the sun was setting. Mark was whittling sharp ends into several straight sticks.

'So, what do you have in mind for those tiny spears?' asked Ray

'I would normally use them to roast marshmallows, but under these circumstances, I might have to roast a bird or frog.' Mark's stomach growled.

'I can see a farmhouse, so I don't think you will have to roast birds or frogs.'

Ray's stomach was growling. It had been more than 24 hours since they had eaten anything.

Once the sun had set and the stars twinkled in the black sky, the two men and their horses slowly worked across the field.

Whoosh. A bird flew up, startling them. They paused for a second to let their hearts calm down, and then they continued.

They first arrived at a barn and quietly opened the doors just enough to let them and their horses inside. Then, they brought down some hay and got a couple of buckets of water. The horses ate and drank.

'Now, it is our turn to get some food.'

Looking both ways, they left the barn and

went to the house. There they were greeted by a friendly dog who wagged his tail. Once inside the farmhouse, the moonlight reflected on rows and rows of quart jars filled with peaches, apple sauce, stews, vegetables, sauerkraut, and pickles. Dried meat, onions, and garlic hung from the rafters.

'This is going to be a feast!'

They chose one jar each of apple sauce, stew, and some dried meat. While traveling back to the barn, they ate some of the dried meat and gave the rest to the dog. Once safely back in the barn, both men took turns slurping out of the stew and apple sauce jars. Then, they drank from the horse's water bucket.

'This is going to be a great night!" They climbed into the loft and rolled out their mummy bags on the soft hay. It was their first good night's sleep in a long time.

* * *

Fritz moved to Johnny's bed sometime in the middle of her story, and now he was on her rag rug. "You're a good dog." She said, gently patting his head.

10 The Hood

Fall disappeared in the night, and the kids were delighted with the winter wonderland that greeted them in the morning. They watched as Dad dug out the van and headed down the long driveway, slipping and sliding. Soon, he'd return with a van full of students, and there would be a fun snow day at school.

"Did you bring your sled?" Johnny asked Hughie as Hughie took his coat off and hung it by the door.

"No, my mom says it will get worn out if the whole school takes turns sliding on it." Johnny nodded; he was one of those kids who loved to take turns on Hughie's sled.

"Well, never mind. We can build forts and play Cowboys and Indians. Or maybe we can find something to slide on," Both boys began thinking. *What would be good to slide on?*

"I'm thinking maybe a cardboard box."

"Or maybe a metal bowl from the kitchen."

"Yeah, both of those might work if we can find them."

"Johnny, could you ask the teacher if she would let us take the reading table outside and turn it upside down so we can slide on it?"

"Great idea!" Johnny eagerly raised his hand.

"Mrs. Dory, can we take the reading table outside at recess and use it as a sled?" Mrs. Dory looked up from her reading class and then at Johnny.

"That's not a good idea!" she scolded, turning back to the students sitting around the table. Hughie and Johnny just looked at each other and shrugged. *It would be fun to go sledding on the reading table.* Turning back to their math workbooks, they were surprised when Mr. Dory entered the room.

"Mrs. Dory, we are going to go to recess a little bit early, and we'll have recess for a little bit longer. This snow is too good to waste." Mrs. Dory slowly closed her teacher's edition to Dick and Jane, rolled her eyes ever so slightly, and then announced.

"OK, children. Please go to the bathroom and put on your snow boots, coats, and mittens." Without a word of complaint, the students jumped from their desks and obeyed.

"Ready?" Hughie wore a ski mask that made him look like a red monster.

"Ready!" The boys shot out of the school doors into the crisp, cold air. And there was Mr. Dory with the car hood from the old Packard and a rope tied around its front latch.

"OK, who wants to try this for a sled and pack us a sledding path down the hill?" Everyone began yelling, "me, me, me."

"We have enough room for everyone, but first, we must prepare the trail. Lower grades jump in, and the big kids and I will pull you to the top. Now, students, just make sure you stay to the sides of the path so your footprints don't make holes in our sledding slope." The students dutifully followed Mr. Dory, and, grabbing the sides of the hood, they pushed while he towed. The eight lower-grade kids hung on for dear life inside the hood and finally arrived at the top, where an apple orchard began. While the bigger boys were stamping out a flat place for the launching pad, the little kids marveled at the red apples that still hung on the tree with clouds of white snow dolloping them like whipped cream.

At last, Mr. Dory said everyone could get in. The first run down the hill was pretty slow; the big boys had to get out and push every so often. But after five runs, the hood slid fast and smoothly and could make it to the leveled area by the school. The ride down was so much fun, but the tow back up the hill was strenuous, and soon, the big kids grew tired of lugging the sled up, so the lower grades decided they'd take the hood up to the top by themselves.

"I want Fritz to have a ride." The little dog had faithfully gone up and then chased the sled down, up and down, until his pink tongue was hanging out.

"That's a great idea! Fritz will go with us this time." All the little kids held the hood while Jenny tried to coax Fritz into the sled.

"Come on, Fritz, yougettogo!" Fritz didn't move, so the kids gave him a push; he resisted and planted his feet in the snow.

"Johnny, can you pick him up and put him in here with me?" Johnny, with the help of the others, heaved Fritz over the side and into the sled, but

"It's going, we're moving!" Jenny screamed, the children tried to stop it, but as hard as they tried to hold onto the sides, the hood began to move down the smooth, snow-packed hill. Some of the students tried to jump in, but their feet slid out from underneath them. Jenny wrapped her arms around Fritz and wiggled to the front of the hood for safety, but that only made the sled go faster. The bigger kids in the leveled part of the schoolyard scattered as she zoomed by. She briefly saw the van

miss her head by a few inches. The hood had never slid this far or this fast. Now, she and Fritz were on the second slope that led down to the fields. She began to feel terror. *Would they end up in the Okanogan River?* Then she heard Mr. Dory.

"Get down, get down, GET DOWN! Pressing herself and Fritz flat against the bottom of the hood, she heard a metallic sound and then felt the barbed wire bounce from the hood and slice through the back of her coat. At last, the hood rested in the middle of the alfalfa field, slowed by the soft snow and buried alfalfa. She and Fritz peeked out from the hood; the school was far up on the side of the mountain.

"Whew, Fritz, that was a close call!" Jenny stood up, shaking the snow off and helping Fritz over the side of the hood, only to plop him into the snow over his head. She could see Mr. Dory and Danny, a lanky eighth-grader, making their way down the hill; she saw him pause at the barbed wire fence and pull off a few tufts of something. At last, they reached her.

"Get back in the hood, and get Fritz too." At Mr. Dory's stern-sounding voice, she couldn't tell if she was in trouble. Dutifully, she picked up Fritz, and they awkwardly slid back onto the cold metallic surface of the hood. Danny and Mr. Dory silently began towing the hood back to the school.

At the barbed wire fence, Mr. Dory paused while Danny pulled the barbed wire up so they could maneuver the hood under. Jenny lay down, cuddling Fritz. She could still see little bits of her coat pinned to the barbs of the wire. *Mom would have to make another repair in her coat of many coats.*

That night, around the supper table, Dad said a prayer of thanksgiving that the barbed wire hadn't hurt Jenny and Fritz. Then, it was never mentioned again. Jenny felt so happy going to bed; she wasn't in trouble after all.

"Hey, Jenny, don't forget Mark and Ray." Johnny's voice was barely heard across the bedroom.

"I haven't forgotten.

* * *

"Mark woke up first and took a piece of straw, gently moved it across Ray's face. There was no response, so he began letting the straw go up Ray's nose.

'Achoo!' Ray woke with a start. Seeing Mark holding the straw, he lunged.

'Now, you're going to get it!' The two men began wrestling, and soon they were stuffing big globs of hay into each other's shirts. Then they heard it.

They stopped their roughhousing and listened again. It sounded as if something or someone was coming into the barn. Ray bent over and looked through a crack in the loft floorboards. A boy of about 10 years old was looking at the horses. He slowly reached out a hand and patted the Palomino. The horse neighed softly, and then the boy reached into his pocket and pulled out a carrot. As he brought it close to the horse's mouth, the horse curled his lips almost in a smile and chopped the carrot almost before the boy could get his hand out of the way."

* * *

Jenny heard the tapping of Fritz's nails as he walked over to her bed. She stopped telling the story and faded into dreamland.

11 The Big Stink

The crystal blue sky cradled a gentle
breeze that danced across the alfalfa fields,
sweeping the sweetest smell into the air.
Fritz had gone to visit Tippy, who was
wagging their tail and sniffing around. They
began to play chase around Tippy's yard;
both dogs stopped abruptly and looked up to
see that Jenny, Johnny, and James had
come outside. Fritz took off, leaving Tippy
alone in his yard. Fritz had made it halfway
through the alfalfa field when a strong smell
caught his attention. A big vulture lifted into
the sky as he ran up to it. *Hmm, this smells
good; I bet Jenny will love it!* Fritz slowly
circled the bloated American Toad. *I just love
this smell.* Fritz bent his neck into the toad;

the flesh sluffed off, revealing green slime. *This is even better!* Now, Fritz made sure that both sides of his neck and part of his torso were covered in slime. *I know Jenny*

will love this.

"Fritz, Fritz, yougettogo." Fritz stopped, then ran as fast as he could, leaving the field and quickly climbing the hill to reach the children.

"P.U., what stinks?" Johnny pinched his nose. As Fritz got closer, the smell became stronger.

"It's Fritz!" Jenny yelled, and the children began running. *Yay, a game of chase,* thought Fritz, and the game was on. The children hightailed it to the back of the school, but Fritz followed. They ran around the car, but Fritz followed. They went to their forts, but Fritz followed. They tried splitting up and running in different directions, but it didn't matter; he would appear. The terrible smell now hung like a heavy curtain in the yard. Mom came up from the apartment and stood at the top of the steps.

"Kids, get in the van . . ." Mom got the words out just as Jenny ran by with Fritz in hot pursuit.

"Jenny, get the tub."

"Johnny, get the hose." Mom started giving orders, and the kids frantically obeyed. Jenny ran down to the basement and grabbed the metal wash tub (she'd just had a bath in it the night before). Struggling, she pulled it up the basement stairs to the side yard. Fritz was still chasing James around the school building.

"Jenny, get the dish soap." Jenny was out of breath but obediently ran back down the steps and got the dish soap. Fritz was still chasing James.

"Johnny, turn on the water and fill the tub." You all promised to be responsible, and now you will wash that STINKING DOG!" Jenny and Johnny began filling the tub; the soap bubbles looked spectacular. Without thinking, Johnny scooped up a handful of bubbles and slung them at Jenny. They covered her face and hair, which caused Johnny to erupt in laughter. Jenny was just about to retaliate.

"Jenny put Fritz in the tub."

"Here, Fritz, here, Fritz, get in the tub." Fritz ignored the order and ran by as he continued chasing James. Jenny finally yelled,

"Fritz, come!" The dog stopped and came to Jenny. She looked at the green slime dripping from his neck and kindly said,

"Fritz, get in the tub." Fritz stared at her, then gave a mighty doggy shake, sending glistening specks into the air.

"Pick him up and put him in the tub." Jenny looked at Mom and then at her pretty, yellow-and-white checkered dress. They had been ready to go to Leanne's birthday party.

"I SAID, PICK HIM UP AND PUT HIM IN THE TUB!" Mom ordered through clenched teeth. Jenny bent down slowly, keeping one eye on Mom while putting her arms around

Fritz's middle. She hugged him close to her body and, using every bit of strength, hoisted him into the tub. Looking down at her yellow-checked dress covered with green slime, she fought back her tears. Now they wouldn't be able to go to the party.

Jenny and Johnny scrambled and fought to keep the squirming dog in the tub. They shampooed him all over and took turns with the sniff test. At last, Mom seemed satisfied and said they should take a shovel, find the dead toad, and cover it up.

"I think we should cover you up, Jenny; you stink worse than Fritz now!" Jenny glared at Johnny.

"Be quiet. You didn't have to carry him."

"Yes, but I did a lot of work."

The two kids let their noses lead the way, and soon found the big dead toad at the edge of the field. One steadied the shovel while the other jumped on the top of the blade. Soon, they had covered the toad with earth, and the children trudged back up the hill.

"Fritz is a lot of work."

"Do you want to give him away?"

"No, I never want to give him away."

"Me neither."

When they reached their apartment, Mom collected their clothes.

"Well, children. How do you like having a dog? The Millers have been asking if we would like to give Fritz to them. They live on a big orchard, far from the main highway, and their kids have fallen in love with Fritz." *Of course, they have; they play with him every day at school. They have all the fun, but none of the work or stress,* thought

Johnny.

"I did hate the smell, and the slime made me gag. But it doesn't change the fact that we love Fritz." Jenny looked at Johnny, they both nodded in agreement. "Besides, he was given to us by God."

"We are still going to Leanne's house. We won't be there as long as we had hoped, but we have presents, and I think you were her only guests."

"Yay, we get to go to the party." Fritz started to wiggle when he heard the words "gettogo."

"Sorry, Fritz, you do not get to go. You are a bad dog." Fritz put his tail between his legs and sat down. He also understood the words 'bad dog'.

"You are staying home and inside." With that, the family left for the party.

After returning home, the kids were soon snuggled in bed.

"Jenny, don't forget where you left off in the story."

"I know, Mark and Ray had seen a boy."

"OK, tell the story; what happened next?"

* * *

"The boy leaned over and picked up the empty jar from Ray and Mark's supper. Slowly, he looked up, and his gaze met theirs. Frightened, he ran from the barn.

'Now we know we aren't alone.'

'I wonder if he is a spy.' The men leaped off the loft and ran after the fleeing boy. They grabbed him, and he began to cry.

'What is it?'

'Don't be afraid. We aren't going to hurt you.'

'Hab keine Angst,' Mark repeated in

German, and the boy stopped crying.

'Wir sind Amerikaner.' The boy looked amazed, jerked away, and ran before they could stop him.

'That's strange. I'm too tired to chase him anymore, and I don't think it is safe to venture out of the barn until it is dark. We'll just have to pray he doesn't tell the wrong people about us. I think we need to get out of here!'

* * *

Just then, Jenny heard the tap of Fritz's nails as he traveled across the linoleum floor to her rag rug.

"Fritz, you were such a stinking dog. Don't ever do that again." Fritz just wagged his tail and licked her hand.

12 The Creek

The early spring sun peeked in through the window. Johnny and Jenny opened their eyes, put on their clothes, and went into the living room.

"Hey Mommy, what are you doing?" Both kids looked as Mom carefully measured hot water and a tablespoon of something into the clear glasses.

"Pee-yewwww, that doesn't smell good." Mom allowed them to smell the tablespoon of clear liquid.

"It is vinegar and it helps the color to go into the egg shells."

James arrived sleepily, and Mom let each kid hold a food coloring bottle and squirt color into a glass. They watched in amazement as the colors swirled into a spiral and spread in a cloudy mist throughout the water.

"Daddy thinks it would be fun if we went to our favorite creek and had our Easter egg hunt there. Quickly eat your breakfast. I packed a lunch, and we're going to have a fun day."

"Does Fritz get to go?

"Yes."

"Yougettogo, Fritz. Yougettogo. Yougettogo." The children shouted at Fritz, and he wiggled with joy!

Each child carefully placed a hard-boiled egg in the glass and waited as long as possible. Then, they lifted the egg out and marveled at the transformation.

"I love my purple one."

"I like my green one."

"I think my favorite one is this orange one."

It wasn't long before all the eggs were colored and packed back in their cartons, and everything was ready to go.

"Come on, kids, we will use the Packard for this trip." After they'd used the hood as a sled during the winter, the hood had been put back on, and it was up and running—that old faithful family car that had taken them on many adventures.

It took the family almost two hours to arrive at their special destination, a creek with a little green meadow surrounded by logs and rocks, perfect for hiding Easter eggs.

"You will sit in the car until Mom and I have all the eggs hidden. And no peeking." The kids obeyed Dad's instructions by lowering themselves onto the car's floorboards.

"Jenny, tell us the story." She thought briefly about where she'd left off the night before and then began.

* * *

"Mark and Ray quickly rolled up their mummy bags and stuffed them in their backpacks with a string, some wire, and an empty jar; all of the items might come in handy. They climbed down from the loft and fed the horses. Silently, they opened the barn doors. Looking both ways to make sure all was clear, they started, when suddenly, something in the bushes moved!"

* * *

"OK, kids, we are ready. The eggs are all hidden." Mom and Dad returned to the car, opened the trunk, and brought out a little basket for each kid. How fun was this? The meadow was filled with patches of color.

"Remember to search for eggs at your eye level or higher and let James find the eggs hidden in the grass."

"That means they've hidden some eggs in the tree," Jenny explained to Johnny.

The children scrambled over the fallen logs, looking under rocks, up in trees, and through the bushes. Soon, each one had a basket full of eggs, and they rushed back to the large quilt Mom had spread out in the middle of the meadow.

"Besides the peanut butter and jelly sandwiches, we can eat our eggs." Mom began handing out the sandwiches and pouring glasses of milk. Each child picked their favorite egg, but when Mom started to crack the shell on Jenny's favorite egg,

Johnny and James decided to pick one they didn't like as much.

The sun was beginning to lower in the sky when Mom and Dad said it was time to go. Everyone piled into the car, and Dad prepared to do the thing he liked to do the most.

"We're going to ford this stream," he announced, and Mom sighed.

"Jenny, how much does a stream cost?" Johnny asked incredulously.

"I have no idea where that question comes from," Jenny replied.

"Dad just said he's going to ford the stream."

"Oh, does that mean that he can afford the stream? Will it be our stream? Will we get to keep it forever?"

Before Jenny could say anything, Dad stepped on the gas pedal, and the car jumped toward the stream, throwing each child firmly against the back seat. Keeping the power to the tires, the car sped through the water, causing waves to splash as high as the windows.

"Do it again, do it again!" Everyone, except Mom, cheered. Dad turned the car around, bumping over the rutted dirt road and easing into the grass that grew along the edges. Then, back onto the road, Dad could get a better start because this side of the creek was facing downhill.

"Hang on!" he shouted as he gunned the motor. Jenny grabbed the armrest and held Fritz, while Johnny and James clung to whatever they could find. They all bounced like jumping beans and yelled in delight when the car hit the water, and this time, the water covered the front windshield. Once on the other side, Dad had to turn on his wipers.

"OK, Paul, that is enough." Dad looked at Mom as if seeing her for the first time. The wipers swished quietly back and forth across the window.

"I'm sorry, Melba. Are you OK?"

"Yes, let's go home."

"Jenny, can you continue the story on our way home?" Whispered Johnny. "What came out of the bushes?"

* * *

"Mark and Ray were so startled that they almost slugged the two kids who had jumped out of the bushes. The boy was the one they had seen earlier. Now he had a girl with him who looked to be his younger sister. Not wanting to waste time, the two soldiers and children quickly moved to the house, getting supplies, blankets, and whatever they could find to pack on the horses.

'Mein nahme iss Ryker, und mein seester iss Hilda,' the boy said with a thick German accent.

'My name is Mark, and this is Ray.' Mark pointed to Ray, and both men smiled.

'Wir müssen zusammenpacken und losgehen.' Mark could speak a little German and wanted the kids to know they had to leave.

'Hund?' The children pointed to the dog.

'No, Hund. We can't have a dog following us that might bark when we need to be quiet.' Ryker looked crestfallen at the phrase *no hund* and went quietly about picking up a few things.

When they left the farm, it was about 6:30 a.m. The children did not look back. No one spoke a word as they continued along the tree line. When they heard motorcycles, they stopped and pressed further into the trees and bushes. As they reached the end of the tree line, Mark motioned for Ray to come closer and whispered.

'Hey, Ray, we should rest here until the

moon comes up. I don't want to take the horses and the kids out into the open field.' Without saying another word, the two men carefully unpacked two blankets and motioned for the kids to rest on one, and they lay down on the other. The horses calmly munched on the grass and flicked their tails now and then at an irritating fly. The day was so quiet and warm that everyone fell asleep. When Mark and Ray opened their eyes, the children were still sleeping soundly, and nestled between them was Hund."

* * *

"I like that Hund found them," Johnny said as he fell asleep, rocking back and forth in the car. The kids didn't remember getting home, Dad carrying each one to bed, or Mom praying by them and tucking them in.

13 Stuck

Jenny watched the raindrops sliding down the windowsills. *Oh no, it would be another day of being unable to play outside.*

"Hey Jenny, what do you want to do at recess?" Huey whispered behind her. *What could one do inside the two-room schoolhouse that had no gymnasium?* Jenny thought.

The two children returned to their desks and tried to finish their math, but all they could hear was the rain. Then, Mr. Dory entered the classroom, followed by the upper-grade students.

"Mrs. Dory, for recess, we are going to play 'Night in the Museum' with both classrooms. I want to go over the rules with everyone:

1. You cannot run, but you can walk quickly.

2. When the Night Watchman looks at you, if you're not frozen like a statue, you must go to the repair shop under the reading table in Mrs. Dory's classroom.

3. You may not make any sound; you can't talk, laugh, yell, or scream.

4. We will take turns being the Night Watchmen, so someone else will become the Night Watchman every few minutes.

5. If the Night Watchman says you have been caught, you can't argue, but most go directly to the basement for repairs (under the reading table in Mrs. Dory's classroom).

6. The only way to get out of the repair shop is for someone to come and "fix" you by

touching your hand before the Night Watchman sees them move.

7. The Night Watchman may not guard the repair shop. But has a certain route to follow.

8. The teachers will be watching the Night Watchman. They must follow the route. He must shine the light and see the "statue" move to call them out.

"We will try these rules; if they don't work, we can change them." Mr. Dory had the students close the blinds, then explained the route and handed a flashlight to the first Watchman, Danny.

"Buzzzzz." The timer went off, signaling that recess was over.

"Recess is over?" All the students groaned.

"Recess was really fun! I just followed the Night Watchman, and every time he turned around, I froze like a statue."

"But it was hard holding perfectly still when the Night Watchman would make funny faces and we would laugh and then have to go to the repair shop."

"Okay, kids. Get back on task and stop talking about recess. I'm glad you had fun, but it's time for our spelling bee."

And that is how the week went - raining every day, but thankfully, Mr. Dory would come up with some fun indoor games. Finally, the weekend arrived, and the sun came out. The sky was so blue, and the grass was so green.

"Mother, I want to take our children and you on a special Sabbath picnic up to the creek."

"Paul, I already have the kids dressed for church."

"No worries, I've already packed them some extra clothes, and you can bring your potato salad and baked beans with some carrot sticks for the picnic."

Church went by quickly, even though it was singing, praying, and preaching. Jenny could use her imagination and think of how fun it would be at the creek.

Once they arrived at the creek, they found the meadow marshy and a raging creek.

"This is awesome!" The kids jumped out of the car and splashed through the mud.

"Maybe we should eat out of the car." Mom suggested.

"Fine with me, I'm starving." Dad opened the trunk, made a table out of the spare tire, and helped Mom divide the potato salad, beans, and one carrot stick on each plate.

"Our Dear Heavenly Father, thank you for this food and for helping it nourish our bodies, Amen. Sit on that log, and I will hand you your food." Soon, all you could hear was the clicking of their forks on the Melamac plate as the children eagerly ate their food, reminiscing about the fun Easter egg hunt they had had the week before, when everything was dry.

"I'm thirsty," announced Johnny.

"You can get water from the creek." Mom handed him a clear plastic cup. He went to the edge of the creek and scooped up some water. It looked murky compared to last week.

"Mom, do you want us to drink dirty water?"

"Let it sit for a moment, and the dirt will settle down, then drink when it becomes clear." Johnny set the glass of creek water down on a flat part of the log. Jenny and James gathered around and stared in amazement as all of the silt and dirt settled to the bottom, and then they each took turns drinking.

"Let's pretend that this meadow is the Everglades with alligators and that we are only safe on the rocks and logs."

"Yes, and Fritz can be the alligator!" As Johnny said the words, his imagination morphed Fritz into a ferocious alligator. He began running to the nearest rock, yelling "alligator" with Fritz chasing him.

Soon, the kids were jumping from rock to log, trying to avoid the 'alligator'. They ran and hollered until they were exhausted and thirsty. Then, they would take their plastic glass to the creek, fill it up again, set it on the log, play some more, and return to a fresh glass of water. In the meantime, Dad played and sang gospel songs while Mom harmonized.

"It's time to go home."

"Can't we stay longer?"

"No, we have things to do, and I'd like to be home by sunset." It was no use arguing. So, everyone wiped their shoes, looked around their Everglades, and piled into the car.

"Hang on." Dad revved the engine, and the Packard sprang forward toward the creek.

"Paul!" Mom got one loud word out before the Packard sank in the middle of the stream and stopped. Dad pushed harder on the gas pedal, and the wheels spun and spun. Dad tried rocking the car back and forth, like he'd do if he were stuck in snow, but it was no use.

"You all just wait here. I'll have us out in no time." Dad began taking off his shoes and rolling up his pant legs.

"Dad, what's that scar on your leg?" Jenny could see the red, thin skin that barely covered his shin bone.

"I'll tell you that story someday, Jenny. But for now, I've got to get you guys out of here." Dad slowly opened the car door. Fortunately, the water came only to the edge of the car's running board. Stepping into the ice-cold water, he winced, slipping on the sharp rocks. Soon, he was back with branches, and Mom was out in the stream helping him put them under the tires.

"OK, Melba, you get in the car and see if it will back up now that we've put these branches under the wheels.

Froom! Froom! Mom tried backing the car onto the branches to get some traction. The children tried not to laugh as they watched the wheels spin water over Dad.

"I need to go potty," James said. And Mom stopped everything and carried him out of the car to the shore.

"I need to go, too," Jenny and Johnny said, and Dad helped them back to the shore. Now, Fritz looked out the back window and began to cry, so Mom went and got him, too.

"We'll use some leverage and be out in no time." Dad lugged one of their long logs over to the car. He and Mom created a lever using a boulder underneath, and soon they were able to raise the back of the car. But the current was so strong that the car swung sideways off the branches, and they had to begin their work again.

"I'm hungry! Is there any food left?"

"Sorry, kids, all we have are carrot sticks."

"These are delicious carrot sticks."

"Hey, where's James?" Mom sounded alarmed.

"He's over there with Fritz," replied Jenny.

"Well, he needs a carrot stick. James, come here and get your carrot stick." James turned slowly around. Bits of food coloring, eggshells, and yolk were all over his face. He smiled with blue teeth as Fritz licked his mouth.

"Oh yuck!" he's eating an Easter Egg from last week. Horrified, Jenny began running to his rescue.

"He probably enjoyed it more than the carrot stick." By now, the sun was setting, and Dad and Mom were exhausted from lifting logs, dragging branches, and doing everything they could to get the car unstuck from the creek.

"Come on, kids, let's get you back in the car, and we're just going to have to sleep in there for the night." Dad went first and laid all the seats down, so the car became one big bed. One by one, they carried each child back to the car, took off their shoes, and then got into the 'bed'. Last of all, Dad sat in the car, dried his feet the best he could, put on his dry socks, and rolled down his pants. Once inside the car, Mom lay on one side and Dad on the other, with all three kids and Fritz in the middle. They covered themselves with the same quilt they'd used the week before to eat lunch on.

"Can Jenny tell us a story, please?" Johnny begged. "She left off last time where Mark, Ray, the two kids, Hilda, Ryker, and the dog, Hund, were fleeing from the Germans."

"Let's see if we can go to sleep without a story," I'll say a prayer." After Dad's prayer, Jenny lay there listening to the water rushing beneath her.

I feel safe in this family sandwich, she thought.

Epilogue

I hope you have had as much fun reading the first in a series of true stories about Fritz and the Dory family as I have had in writing it. I had the opportunity to reflect on the first two years of my school experience and relive the events from a more mature perspective. What I once thought were just

mere circumstances have now become analogous to God's love. I also reconnected with the little church school where these events took place. In recent years, it has been called Peaceful Valley Christian School. The building still stands. But the expense of running a small school has become prohibitive.

Analogous Learning

What is analogous learning, and how can you use it with this book to help your children develop their meta-cognitive skills (thinking about their thinking)? The core of analogous learning lies in the ability to connect the story to deeper social-emotional learning rather than the superficial features that are often found in textbooks and readers. The following are some of the lessons I learned from each story.

Chapter: FANGS

I believe that Satan, the evil one, is like the rattlesnake. He is seeking to hurt and maim just as the snake hurt Fritz.

Chapter 2: Hoped-for Dog

We are often like Fritz; we do all the wrong things, no one likes us, and sometimes we get into trouble when it is not even our fault.

Chapter 3: WHAT'S THAT?

Jenny (the author) learned about God and his care for her dog. This experience served to build her trust in God, which has lasted her whole life.

Chapter 4: Zzzzzip

Sometimes, a consequence, such as losing a privilege or being put on time out, serves a bigger purpose and keeps us from making a life-threatening mistake later on.

Chapter 5: The Pit

When we are tempted by something we think smells, tastes, feels, or looks good, always check with a trusted friend or adult. You would hate to fall into a pit.

Chapter 6: The Spark

Children shouldn't play with fire is an obvious lesson. But my lesson was the generosity of Jenny and how genuinely happy she was to share her few dresses with Emma May.

Chapter 7: The Peanut

James was determined to have his way, to catch the ride and eat; his decision changed his life forever. Think before you act.

Chapter 8: The Man

Whether The Man was real, or James was hallucinating, the message kept the doctor from going directly into surgery with James and resulted in the peanut coming out on its own.

Chapter 9: The Field Trip

Johnny was saved from a painful snake bite because he followed the "directions first-time-given."

Chapter 10: The Hood

Sometimes bad things happen to good people. We will never know if Jenny could have possibly heard the teacher yelling for her to put her head down. I know the sound of the metal hood against the snow was loud.

Chapter 11: The Big Stink

As human beings, we are like Fritz and think that what we are doing will make God happy. But he knows that our motives are actuated by pride.

Chapter 12: The Creek

When families spend time together, free from the digital world, they create bonds that help them withstand tough times later on.

Chapter 13: Stuck

We can feel secure in our Heavenly Father's love, even though we are stuck on this earth.

In book two, **Fritz Finds a Way**, Fritz
continues his

adventures by going
with the Dory family
to another church
school. The school is
bigger and located at
an intersection with a country store across
the road. Now Fritz chases cars, snoops in
places he shouldn't go, saves Jenny from
the Wedding Fountain, gets help when the
new member of the family, Clara, is in
trouble, and discovers doggie jail. Jenny has
to choose between God and Fritz.

About the Author

Dr. Rose Gamblin has dedicated more than 30 years to education, shaping minds for a passion for learning and faith. She is the President and founder of MRG Media Ministries, where she leads an approved and registered virtual high school for homeschoolers as well as a K–12 Homeschool Umbrella program. Dr. Gamblin also hosts the daily radio show *Homeschool Companion*, offering encouragement and practical insights to families across the nation.

In addition to her work in education and media, Dr. Gamblin serves as Grand Canyon University's Faculty Supervisor for the Mid-Atlantic region and as a mentor teacher for international student teachers with Moreland University. Her love for music is evident in her role as Minister of Music at Mt. Nebo United Methodist Church in Boonsboro, Maryland.

Beyond her professional life, Dr. Gamblin treasures time spent with her husband, Michael Gamblin, their four grown children, ten grandchildren, and eight nieces and nephews.